Who is this JESUS we Christians Celebrate?

T.C.C.H. Ministry Curriculum

By

Rev. Dorothy L. Glover

© 2002 by Rev. Dorothy L. Glover. All rights reserved.

No part of this book may be reproduced, stored in a retrieval system, or transmitted by any means, electronic, mechanical, photocopying, recording, or otherwise, without written permission from the author.

ISBN: 1-4033-7642-5 (e-book)
ISBN: 1-4033-7643-3 (Paperback)

This book is printed on acid free paper.

1stBooks - rev. 11/06/02

Unless otherwise indicated, all Scripture quotations are from the King James Version of the Holy Bible. Copyright © 1988, By the B. B. Kirkbride Bible Company, Inc. Used by permission.

With love I dedicate this book to my beloved husband, Joe C. Glover and our children, Sheila, Linda, Joe Jr., and Eleanor, my friend Lorraine R. Offer who encouraged me to persevere in my efforts to finish this manual.

I wish to thank Mrs. Beatrice Cummings for her prayers and support, also Mr. Tesfai Kassye for his encouragement and financial help. I want to acknowledge and thank my special sister-in-law, Mrs. Johnnie M. Glover for her secretarial expertise. I love you!!

TABLE OF CONTENTS

FORWARD xi
COURSE CURRICULUM xiii
COURSE A   Who is this JESUS we Christians Celebrate?... xxi
COURSE B   Who God Is? 3
COURSE C   What is Worship? 15
COURSE D   How to Become God's CHILD? 25
COURSE E   Living in God's Family 37
COURSE F   Growing In God's Family 47
COURSE G   Living in the Kingdom of God 59

WHO JESUS IS
INTRODUCTORY TESTIMONY

I truly believe that if people actually knew better, they would do better, as one of my mentors once said. After breaking through the traditional barriers, and focusing my attention on what the Bible had to say about life, I began to see and to understand who God is and what my purpose on earth as a (Son) child of God. I had to come to grips with the fact that it's not God's book (Bible) plus other books, but it is God's book alone (the Bible). In the contents of God's book it is said, let every man be a liar, but let God be true (Romans 3:4).

I believe the Bible to be the inspired word of God and it is able to make one wise unto salvation through faith which is in Christ Jesus, and is profitable for teaching, for reproof, for correction, for instruction in righteousness that the man of God may be complete, thoroughly furnished unto all good works. (II Tim. 3:15, 16, 17) I learned, through prayer and meditation upon the Word (the Bible) that the world and many churchgoers are deceived as I once was. I also learned that following the traditions of men and allowing society, this Worlds Government to dictate to me how I should live or do this or that, I found myself in bondage and blind to the will and purpose of God for my life. I know now why,

The Bible, God's Word states in Ephesians 4:3 3 - 4 that the worldly men fail to understand that if the Gospel be hid, it is hid to them that are lost, to those who are perishing; in whom the God of this world (Satan, the adversary) hath blinded the minds of them which believe not, lest the light of the glorious Gospel of Christ, who is the image of God, should shine unto them, therefore, I have been inspired to compile a series on WHO JESUS IS.

I have diligently sought the Lord for answers to many questions I had about local church life, it's functions and the behavior of people called Christians. I found the answer in Jesus, the sinless Son of God, and I want to share what the Bible had to say which brought deliverance to me and gave me sight as well as far sight, and vision. Jesus (The Lord is Salvation).

Reverend Dorothy L. Glover

FORWARD

If there isn't any God to establish what is right and what is wrong, the commandment is a human directive that carries no authority.

Thank God for being the Lawgiver who came to earth to redeem the lawbreakers. We need to listen carefully to what God is saying in His word so we can put it into practice.

A Text taken out of context becomes a pretext. How to study the Bible?

>a. OBSERVATION: What does the context say?

>b. INTERPRETATION: What does the text mean?

>c. APPLICATION: What does it mean to your life?

We hope to start our curriculum with a series of courses that relate, emphasize, and teach a definite relationship of cause and effect in knowing God according to His word.

COURSE CURRICULUM

Course A - Who is this JESUS we Christians Celebrate?

Course B - Who GOD Is

Course C - What Is Worship?

Course D - How to become God's Child?

Course E - Living in God's Family

Course F - Growing in God's Family

Course G - Living in The Kingdom of God

Educational Outcomes for The Children's Church Hospital, Inc.

Students will be able to read and understand a variety of literature, for example, the Bible, other educational books, charts, pamphlets, and other resource materials. Skill areas of focus are:

(a) Locating the main idea

(b) Drawing conclusions

(c) Sequencing events

(d) Distinguishing between fact and opinion

Additional skill areas that will be enhanced include:

(a) Oral speaking skills

(b) Writing skills
  (1) Making comparisons
  (2) Using charts and tables to extract information
  Enrichment opportunities will be included in the areas of music and art.

T.C.C.H. MINISTRY

Psalm 119:9

The Children's Church Hospital, Inc.

" A Ministry with a Divine Purpose"

CURRICULUM

Train up a child in the way he should go: and when he is old, he will not
depart from it (Proverbs 22:6).

The Highest Goal of Learning is to know God.

OUR  ARE LIKE A PIECE OF GROUND.

THE GROUND CANNOT PLANT ITSELF WITH A SEED.
SOMEONE MUST PUT THE SEED INTO THE GROUND.

WHEN THE SEED OF THE WORD IS PLANTED IN THE HEART, THE TEACHING OF THE WORD FEEDS IT, AND IT BEGINS TO GROW.

COURSE A

Who is this JESUS we Christians Celebrate?

*WE CHRISTIANS CELEBRATE
JESUS!!!*

THE WORD

THE LOGOS

THE HOLY SPIRIT

THE REVELATION OF GOD TO MEN

This series is designed to help New Believer's in CHRIST, understand the New Life, and become established in the faith once delivered unto the Saints of GOD.

THE STUDY OF THE HOLY WORD

UNIT 1: WHO JESUS IS

OBJECTIVE: As a result of this study, the student will be able to see manifestation of God in Jesus.

1. The Word
   John 1:1-3; Proverbs 8:22; 1John 1:1; Proverbs 8:30; John 17:5; Colossians 1:19

2. The Way
   John 14:5-11; Hebrews 9:8; 10:19,20; John 10:9; Ephesians 2:18; John 14, note verse 7; John 10:9 especially.

3. The Truth
   John 8:32; Romans 6:14, 18, 22; James 1:25; 2:12; 2nd Timothy 3:15-17; John 14:6.

4. The Life, What Is Life?
   John 11:25, 26; 5:21; 6:39, 40,44,45; John 10:9.

THE STUDY OF THE HOLY WORD

UNIT II: A NEW CREATURE

OBJECTIVE: As a result of this study, the student will be able to clearly understand the NEW BIRTH.

1. BEING BORN FROM ABOVE
   Acts 17:22-30; John 3:3, 7, 8; I Peter 1:23; John 3:5-7; Romans 12:1-2.

2. WALKING IN THE NEWNESS OF LIFE
   Romans 6:3-11; Galatians 2:20; Colossians 2:11, 12; Deuteronomy 10:16; Romans 6:6; New life through Christ who is LIFE.

3. WALKING IN OBEDIENCE

   Philippians 2:1-8; Matthew 26:39; John 5:30; 6:38; Hebrews 5:8; I Samuel 15:22-23; Eccl. 5:1; Hosea 6:6; Matthew 5:24; 9:13; Mark 12:33.

4. WALKING IN THE SPIRIT
   Galatians 5:13-26; Romans 6:12; I Peter 2:11; Romans 8:1-14.

THE STUDY OF THE HOLY WORD

UNIT III: ASSURANCE OF VICTORY

OBJECTIVE: As a result of this study, the student should REJOICE.

1. FAITH

2. Colossians 1:2-23; Ephesians 3:17-19; John 15:6-11; I John 5:4, 5.

3. TRUST
   Psalms 37:1-7; Proverbs 3:5, 6; Psalms 118:6-9; Psalms 125:1; Psalms 37:39, 40 (lamb of Zion Rev. 14:1; corner stone of Zion I Peter 2:6).

4. VICTORY
   I Corinthians 15:51-58; I John 5:4, 5; 5:11-15; Victory, a single success or achievement.

* Note: Subject words are defined on page 5
Study course theme song found of page 6

THE STUDY OF THE WORD

Memory Verses for each lesson:

Unit I:
Lesson 1.	THE WORD	John 1:1
Lesson 2.	THE WAY	John 14:6
Lesson 3.	THE TRUTH	John 8:32
Lesson 4.	THE LIFE	John 11:25

Unit II:
Lesson 1.	BEIN BORN FROM ABOVE	John 3:3
Lesson 2.	WALKING IN THE NEWNESS OF LIFE	Romans 6:4
Lesson 3.	WALKING IN OBEDIENCE	Philippians 2:8
Lesson 4.	WALKING IN THE SPIRIT	Galatians 5:16

Unit III:
Lesson 1.	FAITH	I John 5:4
Lesson 2.	TRUST	Psalm 37:3
Lesson 3.	VICTORY	I Corinthians 15:57

THE STUDY OF THE HOLY WORD

Subject Word Definitions

1. Word — Language, Scripture
2. Way — Path, Manner of Life
3. Truth — Fact, Real, Right
4. Life — "Animation, Salvation"
5. Animation — Life, Spirit
6. Being — Existence
7. Born — Brought Fourth
8. Walk — Advance by steps
9. Walking — Moving, Behaving
10. New — Recent, Modern, Fresh
11. Newness — Freshness
12. Obedience — To Submit, Obey
13. Obedient — Submissive, Dutiful
14. Spirit — Sometimes called soul, sometimes called the inner man
15. Assurance — Full Conviction
16. Victory — Triumph
17. Faith — In the theological sense is, intellectually, the assent of the mind to Reveal truth and morality, the submission of the whole man to the requirements of that truth.
18. Trust — Confide in, Rely on.

Note: *The only help we need to teach this series is The Holy Spirit!*

THE STUDY OF THE HOLY WORD

Theme song for the entire course:

Jesus Loves Even Me

I am so glad that my father in heaven tells of his love in the book he has given, wonderful things in the Bible I see, but this is the dearest that Jesus loves me.

Chorus
I am so glad that Jesus loves me, Jesus loves me, Jesus loves me, I am so glad that Jesus loves me, Jesus loves even me.

Who is this JESUS we Christians Celebrate?
T.C.C.H. Ministry Curriculum

God Loves You!

Rev. Dorothy L. Glover

Who is this JESUS we Christians Celebrate?
T.C.C.H. Ministry Curriculum

COURSE B

WHO GOD IS?

Rev. Dorothy L. Glover

Who is this JESUS we Christians Celebrate?
T.C.C.H. Ministry Curriculum

Course B

WHO GOD IS?

The Study of the Holy Word
Out of the mouth of two or three witnesses, the word is established. Matthew 18:166, II Cor. 13:1.

Unit I: Who God is?

Objective: As a result of this study, the student will know and understand God as Creator of the natural universe.

1. Creator Genesis 1: 1; Exodus 20:11, Nehemiah 9:6; Job 26:7, Psalm 24:2,; 33:6; 95:5; 102:25; Hebrews 11:3.

2. Creator of Man Genesis 1:26; 2:7; 5:2; Deuteronomy 4:32; Job 33:4; Psalm 8:5; 100:3; Isaiah 51:13; Malachi 2: 10; Acts 17:28.

3. God the Creator of All Things Genesis 1: 1-31

   Memory verse: Jeremiah 32:27.

4. God is Omnipotent-All-Powerful
   Nothing is too hard for you...
   Psalm 14:3-6; Jeremiah 32:17; 32:27;
   Omnipotence, Is Infinite,

   Job 42:2; Psalm 115:3; 135:6; Isaiah 43:13; Matthew 19:26; Luke 1:37; Revelation 19:6.

   Verse to Remember: I John 3:20.

Rev. Dorothy L. Glover

The Study of The Holy Word

Unit II: The Breath of God

Objective: As a result of this study, the student will understand the power of the Breath of God.

1. The Breath of God
   II Samuel 22:16, Job 4:9; Isaiah 11:4;
   Psalm 59:13; Isaiah 30:28.

2. God imparts the Breath of Life
   Genesis 2:7; Isaiah 2:22; Ezekiel 37:5; Daniel 5:23: Acts 17: 24, 25.

   Verse to Remember: Genesis 2:7.

Rev. Dorothy L. Glover

Unit III: God is <u>Awesome</u>

Objective: As a result of this study, the student will see and understand the awesomeness of God.

Nature teaches us general things about God. God wants us to know him in detail. He gave us a book, the Bible, that tells us what He's like, and more.

1. God is <u>omnipresent-present everywhere.</u> He fills the universe. Jeremiah 23:24 Deuteronomy 4:39; Psalm 139: 8-16; Proverbs 15:3; Isaiah 66:1; Acts 17: 24-28.

2. God is omniscient-He already knows everything. I Samuel 2:3; Psalm 69:5; 139:2; Isaiah 40:28; Daniel 2:22; Matthew 6:8; 1 Corinthians 3:20; 1 John 3:20

3. Omniscience of God
   Job 26:6; 31:4; 34:21; Psalm 147:5.

Rev. Dorothy L. Glover

Who is this JESUS we Christians Celebrate?
T.C.C.H. Ministry Curriculum

The Study of The Word

Memory Verses for each unit

Unit I: Who God Is—Jeremiah 32:27

Unit II: The Breath of God—Genesis 2:7

Unit III: God is Awesome—I John 3:20

Rev. Dorothy L. Glover

Who is this JESUS we Christians Celebrate?
T.C.C.H. Ministry Curriculum

The Study of the Word

Subject word definitions

Awe - a mixed feeling of reverence, fear, and wonder, caused by something majestic, sublime, sacred

1. Awesome - Inspiring awe, showing awe.

2. Breath - air taken into the lungs and then let out. The act of breathing

3. Creator - One who creates God; The Supreme Being.

4. God - Supreme Being; Almighty; Eternal, infinite, all-powerful.

5. Man - a human being; person (homo sapiens)

6. Omnipotent - having unlimited power or authority; all-powerful.

7. Omnipresent - present in all places at the same time.

8. Omniscient - having infinite knowledge; knowing all things.

NOTE: The only help we need to teach this series is the Holy Spirit!

Rev. Dorothy L. Glover

Who is this JESUS we Christians Celebrate?
T.C.C.H. Ministry Curriculum

COURSE C

WHAT IS WORSHIP?

Rev. Dorothy L. Glover

Who is this JESUS we Christians Celebrate?
T.C.C.H. Ministry Curriculum

Course C

What is Worship?

Unit I: What is Worship?

Objective: As a result of this study, the student will understand God our heavenly father is worthy of all glory, honor, and praise.

Can children worship? Yes, indeed. We must provide the proper setting for them to do so. How can they worship if we choose songs that call for hand-flinging motions and borderline shouting? How can they worship if we offer programs of various activities with little or no overall objective?

Let us consider what worship is. What are some of the components of worship? The elements or components are easily identified: singing, praying, praising, giving, and hearing God's Word. But just including some or all of these features in a time frame will not necessarily result in worship. Someone has said, "we can arrange the altar stones, but only God can command the flame from heaven."

What then is worship? Our current word worship is derived from an old English word, worthship, or worthiness. Worship begins with an adequate concept of God—that is, who He is, His worthiness. In Isaiah's book chapter six verse one, Isaiah's experience in the Temple when he stated, "I saw the Lord.... high, and lifted up." The Seraphim declared the worth - ness of the Lord with, Holy, holy, holy, is the Lord of hosts; the whole earth is full of his glory" (v.3). Isaiah responded in reverence, repentance, and obedience.

Rev. Dorothy L. Glover

    Calls to worship?

    Why are we to worship?

    Whom are we to worship?

    What is to be our attitude before God?

1. ATTITUDE

    Psalm 95:6; 96:8 - 9; 99:5; Revelation 14:7; Psalm 18:1, 46, 49; 103:1 - 2.

2. RESPONSE

    We are to worship God because He is worthy of our worship. We worship Him from a heart of love because of who He is and what He has done. Worship, then, is a response of the heart, the inner being, in adoration, praise, thanksgiving and love to God. True worship is a very private experience and cannot be forced on a person.

3. GODLY REVERENCE

    Psalm 4:4; 33:8; 89:7; 111:9; Habakkuk 2:20.

4. HONOR GOD

    Psalm 29:2; 34:3; 57:5; 107:32; Isaiah 25:1; Revelation 19:7.

Unit II: False Worship; Idolatry forbidden

Who is this JESUS we Christians Celebrate?
T.C.C.H. Ministry Curriculum

Objective: As a result of this study, the student will understand worship, true and false.

1. IDOLATRY FORBIDDEN

   Genesis 35:2; Exodus 20:4; Leviticus 26:1; Deuteronomy 7:25; 11:16; 16:22; Psalm 81:9; Isaiah 42:8; I John 5:21

2. IDOLS CHARACTERIZED AS INSENTIENT

   Deuteronomy 4:28; Psalm 115:4. a. Perishable, Isaiah 40:20 b. Helpless, Isaiah 54:20; Jeremiah 10:5 c. unworthy of worship of Intelligent Beings, Acts 17:29.

Rev. Dorothy L. Glover

Who is this JESUS we Christians Celebrate?
T.C.C.H. Ministry Curriculum

The Study of the Holy Word

Memory verses for each unit

Unit I: What is Worship? - Psalm 29:2

Unit II: False Worship - Exodus 20:3

Rev. Dorothy L. Glover

Who is this JESUS we Christians Celebrate?
T.C.C.H. Ministry Curriculum

The study of the Word

Subject word definitions

1. Attitude - a manner of acting, feeling, or thinking that shows one's disposition, opinion.

2. False - not true; in error; incorrect; mistaken.

3. Honor - high regard or great respect given, received, or enjoyed; especially, glory; fame; renown.

4. Idolatry - worship of Idols, excessive devotion to or reverence for some person or thing.

5. Insentient - not sentient; without life, consciousness, or perception.

6. Response - something said or done in answer, reply or reaction, words spoken or sung.

7. Reverence - a feeling or attitude of deep respect, love, and awe, as for something sacred.

8. Sentient - to perceive by the senses of, having, or capable of feeling or perception; conscious.

Note: *The only help we need to teach this series is the Holy Spirit!*

Rev. Dorothy L. Glover

Who is this JESUS we Christians Celebrate?
T.C.C.H. Ministry Curriculum

COURSE D
How to Become God's CHILD?

Rev. Dorothy L. Glover

Who is this JESUS we Christians Celebrate?
T.C.C.H. Ministry Curriculum

Course D

The Study of the Holy Word

How to become God's Child?

Unit 1: Salvation of God

Objective: As a result of this study, the student will understand God's plan of salvation, and how to become God's child.

We are all God's children by creation from a physical perspective; however, as it is written that which is born of the flesh is flesh; and that which is born of the spirit is spirit. God is a spirit. Jesus said unto Nicodemus in St. John's gospel chapter three, except a man be born again, he cannot see (know, be acquaint with, and experience) the kingdom of God, unless a man is born of water and (even) the spirit, he cannot (ever) enter the kingdom of God.

1. SALVATION

    Psalm 27:1; 37:39; 62:2; Isaiah 12:2; 25:9; Jeremiah 3:23; Zephaniah 3:17; 1 Timothy 4:10.

2. ONLY THROUGH CHRIST

    Luke 1:69; 2:30,31; The only door, John 10:9. The only savior, Acts 4:12. His grace is sufficient, Acts 15:11. His blood avails, Romans 5:9,10; 1 Thessalonians 5:9. For the obedient, Hebrews 5:9. At his coming, Hebrews 9:28.

Rev. Dorothy L. Glover

3. CHRIST our, Savior: Came to earth to be savior.

   Luke 2:11; 19:10; John 3:17; Acts 5:31; 13:23; 1 Timothy 1:15; II Timothy 1: 10; Hebrews 7:25; 1 John 4:14 - 17.

4. THE LORD OUR.) REDEEMER

   Job 19:25; Psalm 130:8; Proverbs 23:11; Isaiah 41:14; 43:14; 44:24; 47:4; 59:20; Jeremiah 50:34; St. John 1: 10 - 12.

Who is this JESUS we Christians Celebrate?
T.C.C.H. Ministry Curriculum

The Study of the Holy Word

Unit II: Faith in Christ: Secures Salvation

Objective: As a result of this study, the student will understand through knowledge how faith in Christ secures their salvation.

1. BELIEVING FAITH

   John 3:15; 3:36; 5:24; 6:40; John 11:25; 12:46; 20:31; Acts 8:37; 10:43; 13:39; 16:31; Romans 9:33; 10:9; II Timothy 3:15; 1 John 5:1.

2. SPIRITUAL RECEPTIVITY, James 1:21
   SPIRITUAL DILIGENCE, II Peter 1:10, 11
   SPIRITUAL CLEANSING, Revelation 22:14

Rev. Dorothy L. Glover

Who is this JESUS we Christians Celebrate?
T.C.C.H. Ministry Curriculum

The study of the Holy Word

Unit III: Salvation Possible to ALL Men

Objective: Resulting from this study, the student will understand according to God's word, He is not willing that anyone should perish, but that ALL should come to repentance and be saved.

1. POSSIBLE TO ALL MEN

   Luke 3:6; Acts 2:21; Romans 5:18; 10:13; I Timothy 2:4, Titus 2:11, 12; II Peter 3. -9.

2. THE GIFT OF GOD

   John 3:16; 4:10; Romans 5:15,16; 6:23; 8:32; II Corinthians 9:15; Ephesians 2:8.

Rev. Dorothy L. Glover

Who is this JESUS we Christians Celebrate?
T.C.C.H. Ministry Curriculum

Study of the Word

Memory verses for each lesson

Unit I: Lesson 1. Salvation - Psalm 62:6
Lesson 2. Only Through Christ - John 10:9
Lesson 3. Christ our Savior - II Corinthians 3:11
Lesson 4. The Lord our Redeemer - Isaiah 41:14

Unit II: Lesson 1. Believing Faith - John 3:15
Lesson 2. Spiritual Receptivity - James 1:21
Spiritual Diligence - II Peter 1: 10
Spiritual Cleansing - Revelation 22:14

Unit III: Lesson 1. Possible to all Men - Acts 2:21
Lesson 2. The gift of God - Ephesians 2:8

Rev. Dorothy L. Glover

Who is this JESUS we Christians Celebrate?
T.C.C.H. Ministry Curriculum

The Study of the Holy Word

Subject word Definitions

1. Salvation - a saving or being saved from danger, evil, difficulty, destruction; rescue.

2. Through - passing through: done or proceeding through to the end; omitting nothing; complete.

3. Christ - the anointed; Jesus of Nazareth.

4. Savior - a person who saves; (1) God, (2) Jesus Christ

5. Believing - to take as true, real; to have trust or confidence in.

6. Faith - unquestioning belief that does not require proof or evidence.

7. Receptivity - receiving or tending to receive, take in.

8. Diligence - the quality of being diligent, constant, careful effort; perseverance.

9. Cleansing - to make clean, pure, purge, clean

10. Possible - that can be; capable of existing, can be in the future, that can be done.

11. Gift - something given to show friendship, affection, support; the act, power, or right of giving.

Rev. Dorothy L. Glover

See theme song for the entire courses: Page 6 of course A

Note: The only help we need to teach this series is the Holy Spirit!

Who is this JESUS we Christians Celebrate?
T.C.C.H. Ministry Curriculum

COURSE E
LIVING IN GOD'S FAMILY

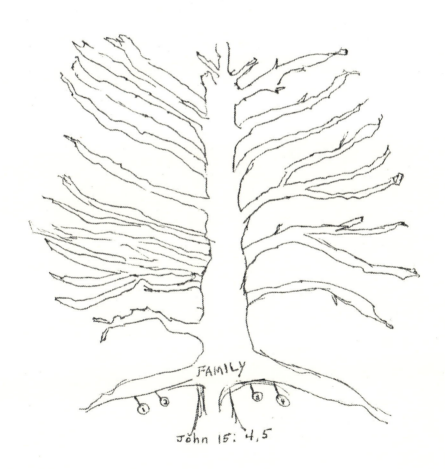

Rev. Dorothy L. Glover

Who is this JESUS we Christians Celebrate?
T.C.C.H. Ministry Curriculum

Course E

Living In God's Family

The Study of the Holy Word

The family - a household establishment, a social unit consisting of parents and the children that they rear, the children of the same parents.

Unit I: Fatherhood of God, Our Father

Objective: As a result of this study, the student will come into the knowledge and understanding of the fatherhood of God.

1. THE BELIEVERS FATHER Through faith we understand that the worlds were framed by the word of God, so that things which are seen were not made of things which do appear. Without faith it is impossible to please him (God): for he that cometh to God must believe that he is, and that he is a rewarder of them that diligently seek him. St. John 1:1-3; 1:12-13.

2. BELIEVERS ADOPTED INTO THE FAMILY OF GOD Deuteronomy 14:2; Isaiah 43:1; 63:16; Ezekiel 16:8; Romans 8:15; II Corinthians 6:18; Galatians 3:26-29; 4:5-6; Ephesians 5:1.

3. ITS SPIRITUAL RELATIONSHIPS OBEDIENCE Secures the Benefits, Matthew 12:50; Luke 8:21 a. Heirship with Christ Entailed, Romans 8:17; 9:26. b. All Barriers Broken Down, Ephesians 2:19; 3:15; Hebrews 2:11.

Rev. Dorothy L. Glover

4. KNOWN AS BRETHREN Matthew 23:8; 25:40; Luke 8:21; Romans 8:29; Hebrews 2:11,17; Revelation 12:10; 19:10.

Memory verse: I John 3:2

Who is this JESUS we Christians Celebrate?
T.C.C.H. Ministry Curriculum

The Study of the Holy Word

Unit II: Special Titles, Children of God

Objective: As a result of this study, the student will understand that they are children of the living God, chosen ones, the Elect.

1. SPECIAL TITLES Matthew 5:9; Luke 20:36; John 11:52; Romans 8:21; 9:26; 1 John 3:10.

2. HEIRS OF GOD Romans 8:17; Galatians 3:29; 4:7; Titus 3:7; Hebrews 1:14; 6: 17; 11:7; 1 Peter 3:7.

3. SONS OF GOD John 1: 12; Romans 8:14; II Corinthians 6:14 - 18; Galatians 4: 7; Philippians 2:13 - 15; I John 3:1

Memory verse: James 2:5

Rev. Dorothy L. Glover

The Study of the Holy Word

Unit III: INHERITANCE

Objective: As a result of this study, the student will see and understand, it's profitable to serve the Lord God, and to be a member of the God family.

1. HERITAGE OF THE RIGHTEOUS (Earthly) Psalm 37:11,22 - 24; Isaiah 57:13; Matthew 5:5; Romans 4:13. (Spiritual) Psalm 61:5; 119:111; Isaiah 54:17; Acts 20:32; 26:18; Ephesians 1:11; Colossians 1:12; 3:24; 1 Peter 1:4.

2. SPIRITUAL RICHES (Enduring) Proverbs 8:18; 10:22; Ephesians 1:5-7; 2:7; Philippians 4:19,

Memory verse: Romans 4:16

Rev. Dorothy L. Glover

Who is this JESUS we Christians Celebrate?
T.C.C.H. Ministry Curriculum

Study of the Holy Word

Memory verses for each unit

Unit I: Fatherhood of God, Our Father - I John 3:2

Unit II: Special Titles, Children of God - James 2:5

Unit III: Inheritance - Romans 4:16

Study of the Holy Word: Subject word definitions

1. Fatherhood - the state of being a father; paternity

2. Believer - to take as true, real, to have trust or confidence (in) as being true, real, good.

3. Spiritual - of the spirit or the soul as distinguished from the body or material matters.

4. Relationships - the quality or state of being related; connection; kinship.

5. Barriers - a fortress, stockade; a thing that prevents passage or approach; obstruction, as a fence, wall.

6. Brethren - (Brother) brothers: now chiefly in religious use.

7. Special - of a kind different from others; distinctive, peculiar or unique; exceptional.

8. Title - inscription, label, a claim or right evidence of such right of ownership.

9. Heirs - a person who inherits or is legally entitled to inherit, through the natural action of the law; right to inheritance.

10. Sons - a boy or man as he is related to either or both parents.

Note: In St. John's gospel chapter 1 verse 12, But to as many as did receive and welcome Him, He gave the authority (power, privilege, right) to become the children of God, that is, to those who believe in (adhere to.) trust in, and rely on) His name, also, Isaiah 56:5, To them I will give in My house and within My walls a memorial and a name better (and more enduring) than sons and daughters; I will give them an everlasting name that will not be cut off.

Who is this JESUS we Christians Celebrate?
T.C.C.H. Ministry Curriculum

COURSE F

Growing In God's Family

OUR  ARE LIKE A PIECE OF GROUND.

THE GROUND CANNOT PLANT ITSELF WITH A SEED.

SOMEONE MUST PUT THE SEED INTO THE GROUND.

WHEN THE SEED OF THE WORD IS PLANTED IN THE HEART, THE TEACHING OF THE WORD FEEDS IT AND IT BEGINS TO GROW.

Rev. Dorothy L. Glover

Who is this JESUS we Christians Celebrate?
T.C.C.H. Ministry Curriculum

Course F

Growing In God's Family

The Study of the Holy Word

It is written in John's gospel, Chapter 8, verses 31 - 32. Then said Jesus to those Jews which believed on him, if you continue in my word, then are you my disciples indeed; And you shall know the truth, and the truth shall make you free.

The Second chapter of the Proverbs, beginning with verses 1 - 6 is a good way to start growing. Now that you know you are a son of God. Thus say the Lord, my son, if thou (you) will receive my words, and hide my commandments with thee (you); so that you incline thine (your) ear unto wisdom, and apply thine (your) heart to understanding; Yes, if you cry after knowledge, and liftest up your voice for understanding; If you seek after her as silver, and searchest for her as for hidden treasures; Then shall you understand the fear of the Lord, and find the knowledge of God. For the Lord giveth wisdom: out of his mouth cometh knowledge and understanding.

Unit I: Growing in God's Family

Objective: As a result of this study, the student will understand spiritual discernment and spiritual knowledge.

1. SPIRITUAL KNOWLEDGE, A cause for Exultation
   Jeremiah 9:24; 31:34; HOSEA 6:3

   Obedience, the condition of receiving; John 7:16 - 17. Liberates the soul from all Error; John 8:31 - 32. Leads to

Rev. Dorothy L. Glover

    Eternal Life; John 17:3; Philippians 3:10 - 14; Colossians 1:10.

2. SPIRITUAL DISCERNMENT I Kings 3:9; Isaiah 7:15; 11:3; I Corinthians 2:14; Hebrews 5:14.

3. EXAMPLES OF SPIRITUAL PERCEPTION (David) II Samuel 5:10 -12; (The Shunammite woman) II Kings 4:8,9; Nehemiah 6:10 - 13; The wise men, Ecclesiastes 2:14; Jesus, Luke 5:22; The Samaritan woman, John 4:19; Acts 10:34.

Memory verse II Peter 3:18

The Study of the Holy Word

Unit II: TRUE WISDOM

Objective: As a result of this study, the student will understand why it is written in Proverbs chapter 3, verse 7, be not wise in thine (your) own eyes: fear the Lord, and depart from evil.

1. THE FEAR OF GOD CONSTITUTES WISDOM Job 28:28; 32:7; Psalm 111:10; The supreme Acquisition, Proverbs 4:7; 9:1; Hosea 14:9; Wisdom lays an Immovable foundation, Matthew 7:24; I Corinthians 2:4 - 6; 12:8.

2. THE SCRIPTURES, THE SOURCE OF WISDOM II Timothy 3:15; 2:15; Full of Spiritual fruits, James 3:17; 1 John 2:20, 21.

Memory verse: II Peter 1: 12

Rev. Dorothy L. Glover

Who is this JESUS we Christians Celebrate?
T.C.C.H. Ministry Curriculum

The Study of the Holy Word

Unit III: Growing in the Knowledge of GOD'S Wisdom

Objective: - To help the student understand, why the fear of God constitutes wisdom.

1. GOD'S WISDOM Psalm 104:24; Proverbs 3:19; Jeremiah 10:6,7; Daniel 2:20; Romans 11:33; 16:25 - 27; I Corinthians 1:25.

2. WISDOM OF CHRIST, as very man Isaiah 11:2; Matthew 13:54; Luke 2:40; I Corinthians 1:24; Colossians 2:3.

3. PRAYER FOR WISDOM II Chronicles 1:10; Psalm 90:12; Proverbs 2:3; Ephesians 1:17; Colossians 1:9; James 1%

Verse to Remember: Job 12:13

Rev. Dorothy L. Glover

Who is this JESUS we Christians Celebrate?
T.C.C.H. Ministry Curriculum

The Study of the Holy Word

Memory verses for each unit

Unit I: - II Peter 3:18

Unit II: - II Peter 1:12

Unit III: - Job 12:13

Rev. Dorothy L. Glover

Who is this JESUS we Christians Celebrate?
T.C.C.H. Ministry Curriculum

The Study of the Holy Word

Subject word definitions

1. Growing - to come into being or be produced naturally; spring up; sprout; to increase in size and develop toward maturity.

2. Knowledge - the act, fact, or state of knowing.

3. Spiritual - of the spirit or the soul as distinguished from the body or material matters; of or consisting of spirit.

4. Discern - to separate (a thing) mentally from another or others; recognize as separate or different.

5. Discernment - an act or instance of discerning; keen perception or judgment; insight.

6. Example - something selected to show the nature or charter of the rest.

7. True - faithful; loyal; constant; reliable; in accordance with fact; that agrees with reality; not false.

8. Wisdom - the quality of being wise; power of judging rightly and following the soundest course of action, based on knowledge, experience, understanding.

9. Fear - a feeling of anxiety and agitation causes by the presence or nearness of danger, evil, pain, etc.

10. Constitutes - to set up; establish; to be actually as designated. To set up (a law, government, institution, etc.)

Rev. Dorothy L. Glover

11. Prayer - the act or practice of praying, as to God; an earnest request; entreaty; supplication.

The only help needed to teach this series is the Holy Spirit!

Who is this JESUS we Christians Celebrate?
T.C.C.H. Ministry Curriculum

COURSE G
Living in the Kingdom of God

Rev. Dorothy L. Glover

Who is this JESUS we Christians Celebrate?
T.C.C.H. Ministry Curriculum

Rev. Dorothy L. Glover

Who is this JESUS we Christians Celebrate?
T.C.C.H. Ministry Curriculum

Course G

Living in the Kingdom of God

The Study of the Holy Word

St. John chapter eighteen, verse thirty six, Jesus answered, My kingdom is not of this world: if my kingdom were of this world, then would my servants flight, that I should not be delivered to the Jews: but now is my kingdom not from hence (here). The kingdom of God cometh not with observation: Neither shall they say, Lo here! For behold the kingdom of God is within you. (Luke 17:20-21)

Unit I: TIME SEEKERS, or with outward show.

Objective: As a result of this study, the student will see and understand, that the things that are seen are temporal; the things that are not seen are eternal.

1. Acts 1:6, 7; Luke 17:20; Matthew 24:3; Mark 8:11,12; John 2:18; 3-6.

2. KINGDOM OF GOD Matthew 12:28,29; 3:2; 4:17; 10:7; Luke 21:31.

3. PREACHING OF THE KINGDOM OF GOD Mark 1:14; Luke 4:43; 8:1; 9:2; 16:16; Acts 1:3; 8:12; 28:23,24.

Verse to Remember: John 3:5

Rev. Dorothy L. Glover

Unit II: KINGDOM, SPIRITUAL

Objective: As a result of this study, the student will know what the Word of God says about the kingdom of God.

1. SPIRITUAL KINGDOM Romans 14:17; II Corinthians 4:20; 15:50-54.

2. CONDITIONS OF ENTRANCE, into (Heavenly kingdom) Humility, Matthew 5:3,10; Sympathetic service, Matthew 25:34 - 35; Perseverance, Luke 9:62. New Birth, John 3:3; Endurance, Acts 14:22; II Thessalonians 1:3 - 6; Faith and Love, James 2:5.

3. GOD'S KINGDOM COMING WITH POWER Daniel 2:44; Mark 9:1; *Acts 2:2, 3, 4; I Corinthians 4:20; Revelation 11:17; 12:10; 19:6.

4. ETERNAL KINGDOM OF GOD and CHRIST Isaiah 97; Daniel 4:3,34; 6:26; 7:13 - 14,27; Micah 4:7; Luke.33; II Peter 1:11; Revelation 11:15.

Verse to Remember: Deuteronomy 33:27

Who is this JESUS we Christians Celebrate?
T.C.C.H. Ministry Curriculum

The Study of the Holy Word

Memory verses for each unit

Unit I: Time Seekers - John 3:5

Unit II: Kingdom, Spiritual - Deuteronomy 33:27

Rev. Dorothy L. Glover

Who is this JESUS we Christians Celebrate?
T.C.C.H. Ministry Curriculum

The Study of the Word

Subject word definitions

1. Living - alive; having life: not dead, full of vigor; in active operation or use.

2. Time - indefinite, unlimited duration in which things are considered as happening in the past, present, or future; every moment there has ever been or ever will be.

3. Seekers - to try to find; search for; look for; to seek the answer to a question; to look for someone or something.

4. Kingdom - a government or country headed by a king or queen; monarchy; the spiritual realm of God.

5. Preaching - to speak in public on religious matters; give a sermon to advocate by or as by preaching; urge strongly or persistently.

6. Conditions - anything called for as a requirement before the performance or completion of something else; provision; stipulation; anything essential to the existence or occurrence of something else.

7. Entrance - the act or point of entering to make an entrance; a place for entering; permission, right, or power to enter; admission.

Rev. Dorothy L. Glover

8. Eternal - without beginning or end; existing through all time; everlasting, forever the same; always true or valid; unchanging.

*Note: **The only help we need to teach this series is the Holy Spirit!***

Printed in the United States
905100004B